Pissing Women

CHEERIO

CHEERIO

First published in Great Britain in 2025 by
CHEERIO Publishing
www.cheeriopublishing.com
info@cheeriopublishing.com

Cover photograph: Sophy Rickett

Design: CLEO Studio

A CIP catalogue record for this book is available from the British Library.

ISBN: 9781917283090

Pissing Women

Praise for Sophy Rickett

'Sophy Rickett is destined for great things. Her photographs of women pissing (upright) against London landmarks appropriate an exclusively male act of public freedom. Part desire . . . part social commentary, Rickett mixes the comic with the seditionary. Forget your better judgment and head for high rise enlightenment.'

Tania Guha – *Time Out,* 1995

'Rather than in *Bad Girls* where being bad was enjoyable, Rickett's pissing looks like a sober undertaking. These girls piss in the city because that's what they always do, there's no need to smile about it. More so, the triptych, women in suits, the three graces, whatever, is a projection of the kind of banal situation women find themselves in when they're waiting for men doing the same. Rickett's iconography anticipates deconstruction. Its clear rootedness in the ongoing semiotic enquiry around the gaze, cinema, photography desire and power somehow still leaving it looking, in one visitors eyes, 'like an advert'.'

Pauline Van Mourik Broekman – *Mute,* 1995

'Why can men pee in public when women don't dare to? And why can't we share that furtive bravado of the caught-short male? The dark pools in Rickett's photographs are the urban excrescences we step to avoid, viscosities we don't mention, adverse signs of life on the hard grimy surfaces of walls and pavements. Like looking down and wondering what I might be like to fly, this is a taboo subject . . . Rickett's piece is a rumbustious comedy as fitting for a billboard as a gallery, a good big satire with a potent political edge.'

Val Williams – *Creative Camera*, 1996

‘How could this choice of subjects allow the artist to explore the experience of being looked at? Is it our own gaze as viewers that is being addressed? Rickett’s early series of night-time photographs *Pissing Women* might invite this kind of interpretation. Women dressed in slick business suits were depicted peeing in City locations, standing upright like men. The pictures had a certain shock value and were widely reproduced. The viewer became a spectator to an intimate, private event, yet the posture and public display of the women seemed to undermine any voyeuristic position and return the objectifying gaze.’

Darian Leader, 2016

‘Sophy’s practice has evolved into something quite different in the decades since the photos were taken. But, her interest in disrupting patriarchal and institutional structures persists. As *Pissing Women* is given new life in 2023, it still feels shocking. It still feels relevant. And it’s still fucking funny. In the end, it’s a reminder of how the same cultural conversations – about gender, ownership, performance and consumption – rematerialise in different packaging across generations. Same piss. Different toilet. (Or a different wall to spatter it up.)’

Flossie Skelton – *iD*, 2023

‘In a boisterous act of rebellion, Rickett and her friends dressed up in their skirt suits and heels, and posed for photographs while urinating on the streets of London. Here, Rickett can be seen on Vauxhall Bridge, the headquarters of MI6 looming in the background.’

Gabrielle Schwarz – *The Guardian*, 2024

CONTENTS

Vauxhall Bridge, 1995

PUBLISHERS' NOTE

It's 1994 and the City, London's financial centre, is pulsating with new energy. The yuppies of the decade before are more subtle now — the ubiquitous mobile phones they now carry an obvious marker of the move from analogue to digital.

As Britain crawled from economic recession towards a brighter and more hopeful future, Sophy Rickett had embarked upon an artistic project that would come to define an era, challenge societal norms and provoke new conversations about space, gender, visibility and performance.

This simple yet defiant gesture disrupted the carefully guarded boundary between public and private, masculinity and femininity, and subverted the very norms that dictate who is afforded the opportunity to occupy space and how.

Three decades on, *Pissing Women* continues to

resonate. As we celebrate the 30th anniversary of this formative work, its relevance has only deepened. Raw and immediate, Rickett's project not only encapsulates the rebellious spirit of its time but also speaks to ongoing struggles around gender identity, bodily autonomy, the visibility of women in public places, and the accommodations made for female bodies in traditionally male-dominated spaces. By photographing herself and her friends in these intimate yet transgressive moments, Rickett shifted the gaze and reclaimed the narrative around female bodies, exploring how space, power, and femininity intertwine.

This new edition of *Pissing Women*, published by CHEERIO in 2025, brings fresh perspectives from contemporary female artists and writers, offering personal and creative responses to Rickett's provocative images. Renowned choreographer Holly Blakey, acclaimed film director Sophie Fiennes, multi-media artist Chila Burman MBE and

OUTTAKE FROM VAUXHALL BRIDGE SHOOT

musician St. Vincent among others reflect on how the project's themes intersect with their own work and experiences, layering their interpretations with Rickett's own exploration of identity, memory, and time. Together, these voices spark a vital dialogue that pushes the boundaries of art and gender politics.

This book contains the three central images from the 1995 *Pissing Women* exhibition, as well as photographic plates, outtakes, and contact sheets recovered from the cutting room.

Clare Conville & Harriet Vyner

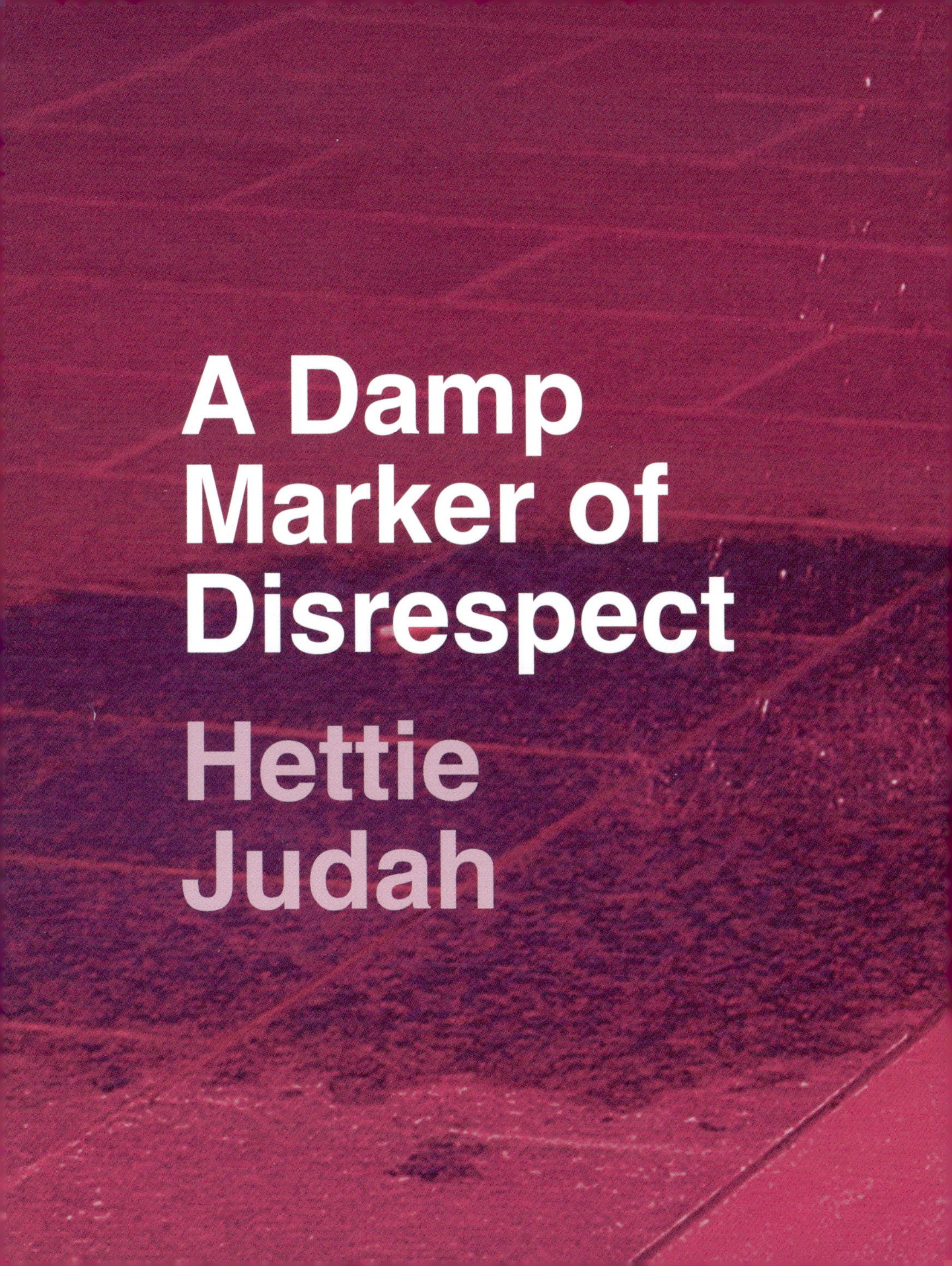

A Damp Marker of Disrespect

Hettie Judah

A DAMP MARKER OF DISRESPECT

HETTIE JUDAH

The arc is enviable. The puddle, impressive. Such control. Such capacity. These women piss like gunslingers, shooting from the hip, shoulders curled, weight in their heels. They're in corporate drag, skirt suits that perform like cloaks of invisibility in central London. It's a uniform that allows them to hide in plain sight, subversive intent concealed beneath the disguise of cubicle drones fresh off the late shift. At Broadgate Circle in London's financial district, security guards pass and pose with a young woman on the steps of a flashy office block. In a black jacket and skirt, glossy hair pulled back off her face, it is inconceivable that this 'baby yuppie' is responsible for the ample puddle adjacent.

And yet she is.

Pissing on London's corporate and civic infrastructure is both a territorial gesture and a subversive one. This piss splashes totems of patriarchal authority. Visible behind Rickett at the end of Vauxhall Bridge is a postmodern ziggurat, home to MI6, Britain's Secret Intelligence Service. All 17 chiefs of the Secret Intelligence Service have been men. In the early 1990s, so few women held senior positions in British companies that John Major's government launched Opportunity 2000, a scheme pushing hopelessly for gender parity by the new century. Rickett's protagonists leave their marks on an overbearing cityscape not built for their bodies or their needs – not least in the failure to provide enough women's lavatories. They are spiritual offspring of that wild punk VALIE EXPORT, who contorted her body around the imperial architecture of 1970s Vienna and fly-posted the city with pictures of her defiantly exposed muff.

In 1981, Dawoud Bey photographed art world iconoclast David Hammons urinating on a looming steel sculpture by Richard Serra. In his pomp, Serra was the macho daddy of New York sculpture, expanding across public space with monstrous structures that flexed the blue-collar associations of their weathered steel. Excluded from the mainstream of New York's art world at the time, Hammons's was a retaliatory gesture from a black outsider: pissing in. Pissing is a rebel gesture, the coarse recourse of the powerless, a damp marker of disrespect.

There is a bawdy heritage of painted pissers in Dutch genre paintings. Judging by the number in the Royal Collection, British monarchs must have laughed like drains at these drunken peasants relieving themselves. Look for them at the margins of party scenes, they are comic relief to reward the observant viewer. Unlike the piddling Dutchmen, Rickett positions her *Pissing Women* at the proud centre of things. Comic but not apologetic, relieved but in control.

OUTTAKE FROM VAUXHALL BRIDGE SHOOT

OUTTAKE FROM VAUXHALL BRIDGE SHOOT

The early 1990s were a pissy time in the art world. In the summer of 1994, London's Serpentine Gallery showed Helen Chadwick's *Piss Flowers*, sculptures cast from piss holes in the snow. Their frilly petals were formed by the guided stream of her partner David Notarius, while the proud and phallic pistils were moulded from deep holes bored by jets of Chadwick's urine. Throughout the decade, scandal streamed around Andres Serrano's *Piss Christ* (1987), a photo of a plastic crucifix immersed in urine, illuminated by a golden shaft of light. Serrano was accused of blasphemy, and *Piss Christ* vandalised, censored and attacked with hammers. The hysteria was rooted less in Godliness than the anxiety provoked by bodily fluids during the AIDS crisis. Liquid transgressing the boundaries of the body carried associations of contamination.

Urinating is a function of the animal body. For women, it is an act supposedly confined to the private realm, together with all other functions that threaten their fetishised purity as objects of

OUTTAKE FROM VAUXHALL BRIDGE SHOOT

desire. The fantasy of feminine perfection did not arrive with the invention of the airbrush and the indoor loo. Already in the 1730s, Jonathan Swift satirised the public desire to be hoodwinked by the flawless public persona of a woman who, like all mortals, must surely sweat, snot and seep. At the climax of *The Lady's Dressing Room* Strephon opens the lid of his beloved's chamber pot and is shocked to discover she possesses a functioning bladder and digestive system.

More fool he, thinks Swift's narrator: '*Should I the queen of love refuse, / Because she rose from stinking ooze?*'

Women don't always piss in private. Un-ladylike behaviour takes place in the Ladies. Witchcraft happens in the gossip between cubicles – the exchange of information, the passing of judgement, the sharing of secrets. Rickett's *Pissing Women* are engaged in a modern form of anasyrma: a ritualistic raising of the skirts. It is an expression of female power and defiance, the flouting of social codes. The night streets are not thought safe for young women, but Rickett's tribe are armed with a camera and full bladders.

In the enchantment of the act itself – this standing nocturnal piss – the city of the patriarch discovers itself possessed.

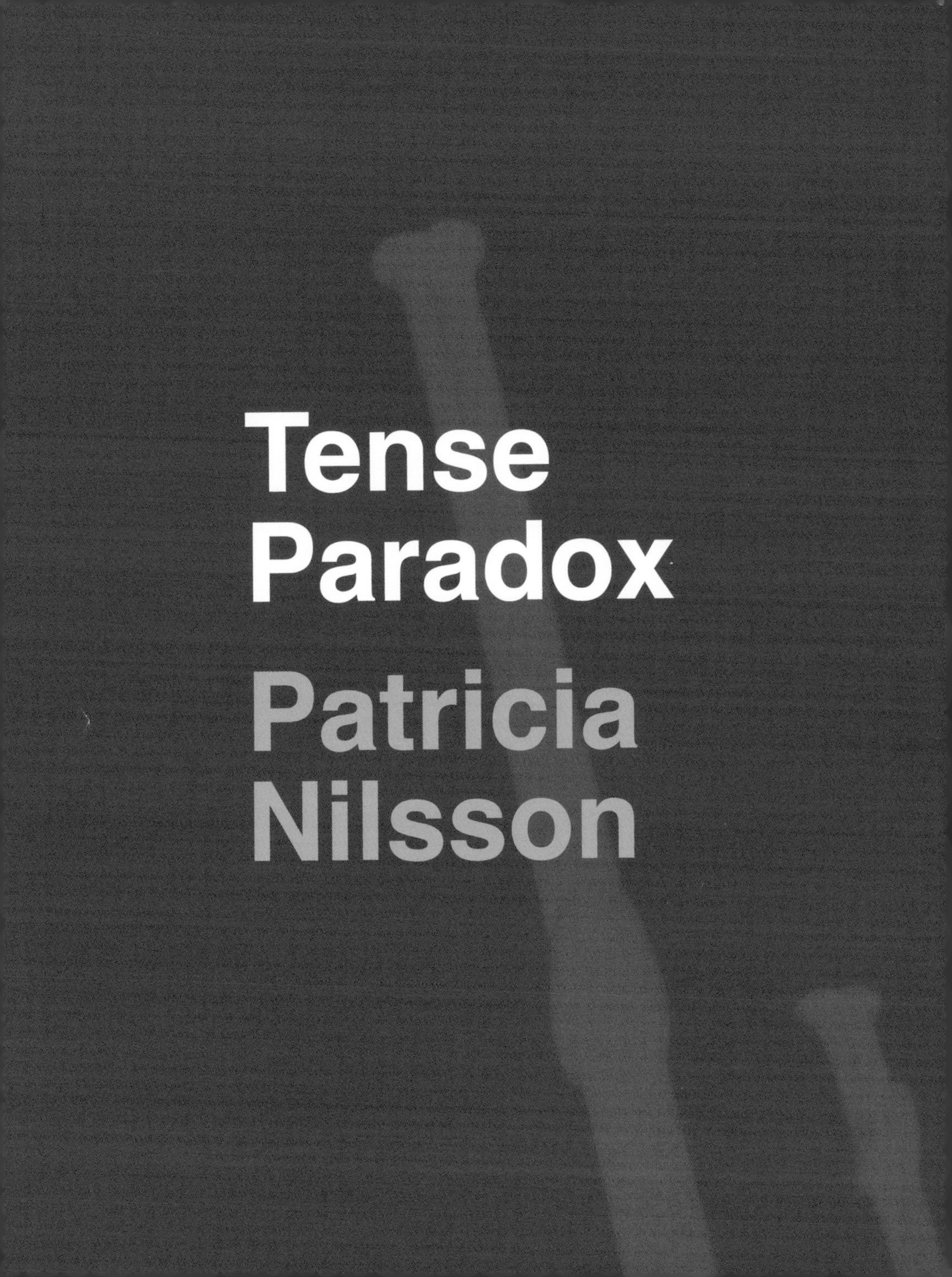

Tense Paradox

Patricia Nilsson

TENSE PARADOX

PATRICIA NILSSON

When men piss in public, they claim space. A quick turn toward a wall; a casual zip; a canine mark of territorial dominance.

For women, it's a different story. Relieving oneself in public becomes an exercise in invisibility – ducking into shadows, crouching behind bushes, making ourselves small to avoid being seen. 'Women's bodies, with all their perceived mystery, are meant to remain private – they are defined by modesty and decorum, hidden until purposefully displayed in the service of beauty or pleasure.'

The image of Sophy Rickett, in a grey pencil skirt suit, pissing on Vauxhall Bridge, reminds us how provocative it once was to suggest that woman, in her quest for a place in the capitalist world, could act like a man among men. It is a time capsule. Thirty years on, the transgressive image of a woman unapologetically taking up space has been absorbed into a hollow corporate feminism – pantsuit girl boss! – that insists on conformity rather than liberation. Women now should behave like men in order to succeed. The demand has changed form – from modesty to mimicry – but the expectation to conform remains unchanged. It is a tense paradox: some of the rules have changed, but the expectation to obey remains.

Something that has not changed is that a woman in public automatically forfeits the virtuosity associated with her imagined private sphere, which is why these images are so provocative. It has something to do with the non-linear continuum '. . . between the vulgar and the erotic, endpoints on an amorphous spectrum of judgement that women know all too intimately.' By showing in public something that female bodies are only meant to do in private, Rickett transfers the burden of policing onto the viewer, forcing them to grapple with the discomfort of judgement. Is this woman dangerously out of control?

TEST SHOOT AT BROADGATE CIRCLE

Or, worse, is she trying to arouse attention and favour from men? 'Assigning intention is for the viewer to worry about. Rickett clearly doesn't give a piss.'

How absurd that the mundane and universal act of urination remains so shrouded in taboo! Yet, it's hardly surprising: anything that evokes the primal desires of the animal within tends to riddle us with self-consciousness. It is our great capacity for shame – one of humanity's defining traits – that ultimately polices our bodies, dictating what is acceptable and what is not in both public and private life. Breaking taboos holds revolutionary potential. By flagrantly defying the rules that dictate what women are supposed to do, this photo series compels its audience to consider the foundation that these norms rest on. The pissing woman, against a backdrop of cold, corrupting concrete, forces us to reconsider what we truly find polluting: the natural act itself, or the societal rules that govern it. The artist leaves us with an uneasy question: is it the act itself that unsettles, or the defiance of the rules that demand it remain hidden? The woman pissing, exposed yet unbothered, forces us to confront the arbitrary boundaries drawn around bodies and behaviour – lines that have shifted but never disappeared.

These photos don't offer answers. Instead, they dwell in the tension, reminding us that the pursuit of liberation often risks becoming a mere exchange of one set of rules for another.

The Bottle

Juno Calypso

THE BOTTLE
JUNO CALYPSO

I wish I never needed a toilet again. The toilet should need me.

I don't like piss. I don't like pissing in the street. I don't even like pissing in my own house.

It would be nice to wake up with the kind of crackpot anatomy the world wants to believe women are in possession of. No plumbing, no gas, no sewage system.

Not only are we women expected to upkeep this fiction, the only way seeemingly to free ourselves from it is to be loud and radical about something that stinks.

No, I don't want to be piss positive. Even those people who think drinking it is somehow healthy pinch their noses.

OUTTAKE FROM OLD STREET SHOOT

OUTTAKE FROM OLD STREET SHOOT

It was as a teenager, underage in a nightclub, that I was first exposed as a piss prude. Having waited in the line for the toilet together, Laura invited me to share her stall.

One of the consequences of women being confined to individual cubicles is how much longer our queues become. It often makes much more sense therefore to go in together. You might, for instance, be on drugs, desperate to avoid the risk of getting lost or confined to a cramped space with your own thoughts. The logic, however flimsy, is based on companionship. A bit like using a self-checkout with your friend, but paying with separate cards.

Laura was blessed with a knack for imitating adult behaviour much more skilfully than me. She went for drinks with 'the girls' and called everyone 'babe'. She greeted new people with air kisses. When Laura swore at her parents, they wouldn't throw her out the window; they'd laugh.

I locked the metal toilet door behind us and instinctively turned to face the wall as Laura began unbuttoning her jeans.

This, it turns out, is terrible cubicle etiquette.

"*You know you don't have to do that, Juno.*"

The gig was up. She was laughing at me.

. . . And I'd done everything so well up to then. I'd inhaled the cigarette smoke, swallowed the pills, downed the shots.

But it was here, in the ladies room, that I fumbled.

In that moment, I was exposed as an inhibited woman. A lady in the land of ladettes. How was I supposed to know you were meant to watch the piss? That, while you were allowed to ignore it, you mustn't turn away from it apparently.

I learnt the importance of maintaining eye-contact, then. That we each had a duty to keep the flow of both conversation and urination steady.

It is traditional amongst women to turn to one another and recite ancient female proverbs – "*That's disgusting!*", "*I wish we could do that!*", "*It's not fair!*" – when happening upon a man relieving himself in public.

A boring person might call this penis envy. As if it were foolish to want to know what it's like to prematurely ejaculate, or get your genitals out in public without being called a whore.

The thing is, however: we *could* do this if we wanted to. Sophy's photographs prove it. *They* just don't want us to. *They* want to keep us on the 'urinary leash', confined to the home. The British government only introduced public toilets for women because it kept us shopping for longer.

There is one thing we can't do, though.

You know what we can't do? We can't piss in bottles. And I'm grateful for that.

I'll never know what it feels like to go into a shop, browse the shelves and think *yes, that'll do – my new toilet.*

I should say now that I'm not talking about the desperate man. The delivery man, or the Van Man. The man without a choice. I'm talking about the Bedroom Man. The man who keeps warm bottles beneath his bed. *Why go down the hallway when the tip fits so well in this plastic rim?*

Perhaps this is in fact an advantage. No matter how depressed you become, you know that you'll always have to get up eventually.

Never a bottle. The bottle never tempts me.

I'll never desecrate the bottle.

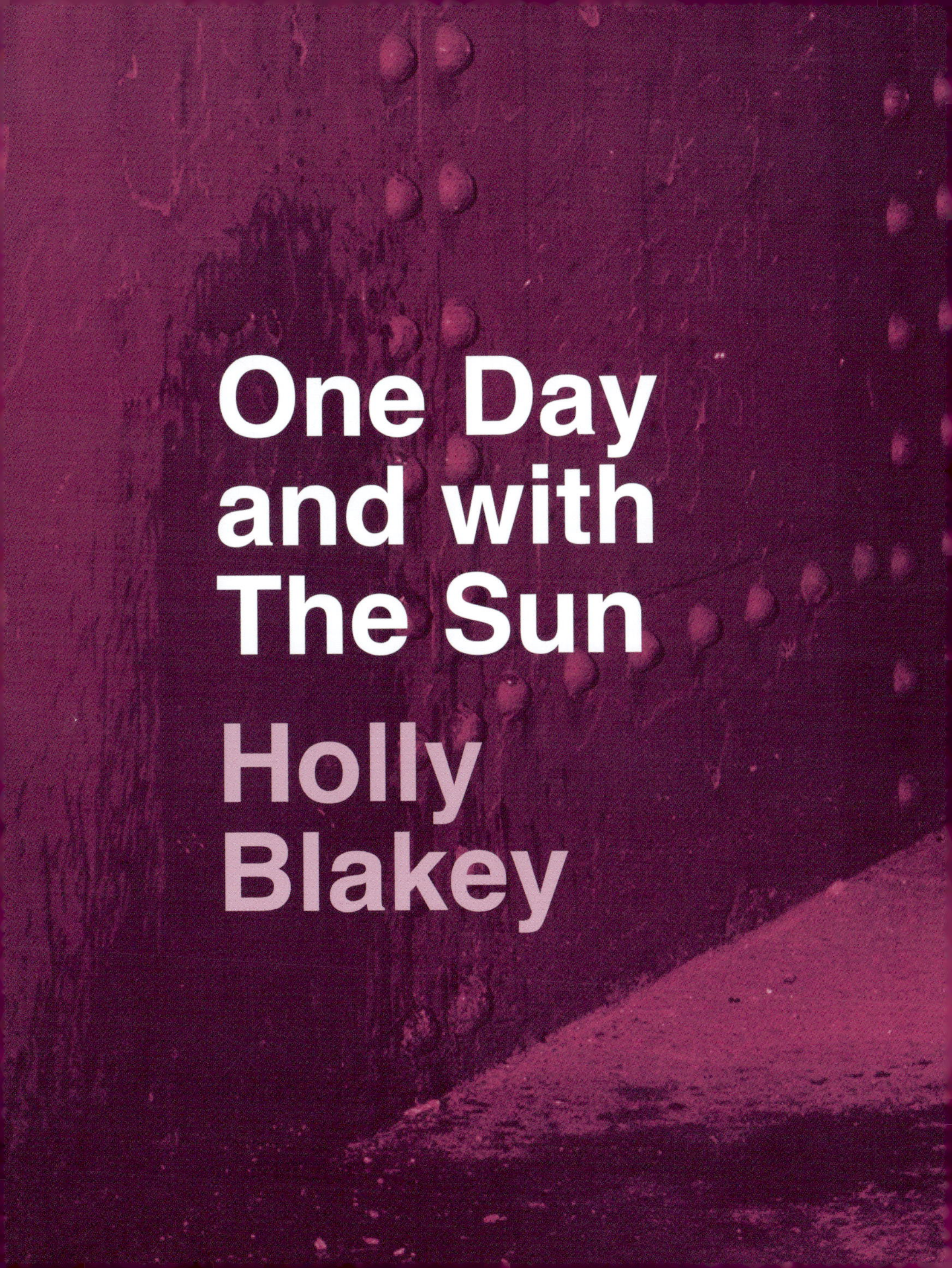
One Day and with The Sun
Holly Blakey

ONE DAY AND WITH THE SUN

HOLLY BLAKEY

Just yesterday, London in the summer, I saw a man pressing his body quietly against a wall outside the tube in Vauxhall. 'There was a perversion to his resting forehead on the warm brick, and an uncertainty, I suppose, to his physical lengthiness. Tall, slim, smartly dressed, his body was totally upright, his feet parallel – though turned out, left and right, a tiny bit.'

As far as I could tell, the man was unaware of my watching eyes. It was his nearness to the wall that struck me. The intimacy of it, his hand and his piss. He conveyed a kind of careless self-importance: the sun on the back of his head totally unromantic.

I can do that too! I remembered. Pissing standing up. I have tried before, a couple of times with my sister at Glastonbury.

TEST SHOOT AT BROADGATE CIRCLE

edge of the festival perfectly pissing, teeth glinting white in the sunlight under a cloudless sky.'

I remember it! And now as I consider this photograph I almost feel sad. Was I pretending to harness something way beyond pissing? was I even in on the joke?

The women in Rickett's series reach forward with their pubic bones, towards their noses, encouraging their knees to bend in a posture that reads uncannily like power and celebration. There is no vulnerability, no self-indulgence here whatsoever.

Immediately collective and playful, these figures beg me to ask whether others see more than one woman in each of these portraits? Perhaps I just want to be in on the message, in on the untowardness of their rebellion, the spilling of something, the staining of the ground . . .' The photographs' collective motif is a noisy exhalation where high heels almost tamper with the joke but don't succeed. An unruly 'I will piss fucking here and there and anywhere' and in this cascade, in this moment I can be reminded of the weighty cosmic potential I hold in my body, and smile by the light of the moon. Or with the sun on the back of my head.

Silvertown, 1995

Diligently Doing It

Sophie Fiennes

DILIGENTLY DOING IT

SOPHIE FIENNES

To piss standing up works beautifully as a metaphor, even if the physical event is likely a messy debacle engaged in only by the curious, intrepid or desperate: women generally squat.

Pissing Women are brazen girls who stand and squirt streams of urine in nocturnal, urban public places, marking a patch and leaving a stench. Frozen in time, blended threads of piss are human fountains caught in photographic flashlight. In narrative terms, these images suggest ecstatic release on a drunken night out after a day at the office.

But *Pissing Women* piss with intent and their faces are serious. They are diligent to the task. They do not wear trousers, but boxy skirts that limit their aim. Little girls, young faces; *Pissing Women* are on the cusp of daring, not quite in a state of wild abandon, but doing

OUTTAKE FROM OLD STREET SHOOT

OUTTAKE FROM OLD STREET SHOOT

it nonetheless. It's dangerous for women to piss in public. Pissing leaves a stain and it's a shame. It's shameful. It's dreadful how hard and complicated it can be for women to piss in public. The metaphor here is the leaving of a stain.

Jane Austen, we are told, wrote her books on small bits of paper she could quickly hide and slip under the blotting pad as she was, 'careful that her occupation not be suspected by servants, or visitors, or any persons beyond her own family party,' and a swing door which creaked when it was opened 'gave her notice when anyone was coming.' She was secretive about her writing and withheld her name, but not her sex. Her books were published as, '*By a Lady*'. Like other eighteenth century female creatives, making work in world dominated by male privileges brought with it the weight of stain-shame and anxiety. Historically much has changed, but it's still hard to hold the pen.

Trolls gather quickly, and decisions have to be

made on where to draw the line between sense and sensibility, between independence and prey. Being a woman is fraught and freaky; there's so much more that comes out of our bodies than words. The P in pissing is strong; the consonant sets it off with vigorous flourish. It's not hissing or kissing. Being pissed is also to be drunk. Patti Smith is intoxicated by language, panting out the lines in her early masterpiece, *Piss Factory* from 1974:

'Sixteen and time to pay off
I get this job in a piss factory
Inspecting pipes . . .'

Caught between the sweat and drudgery of female factory work and the complacent calm of the convent nuns that she spies on, Smith is ready to topple feminine monoliths as she grasps at her punk drive, her 'Mustang' energy, that causes the over-production that is 'screwing up the quota.' She wants to smell the way boys smell, 'that forbidden acrid smell.'

OUTTAKE FROM OLD STREET SHOOT

Frenzied, the words push and gush out of her:

'And I got something to hide here
Called desire
I got something to hide here
Called desire
And I will get out of here.'

'The free woman is just being born; when she has won possession of herself perhaps Rimbaud's prophecy will be fulfilled,' Simone De Beauvoir writes in *The Second Sex*. She is citing a letter Rimbaud wrote in 1871 in which he foresees a future where women's unmeasured bondage shall be broken, 'She will come upon strange, unfathomable, repellent, delightful things,' he writes.

Pissing Women, the series of photographs by Sophy Rickett from 1995, is one such thing.

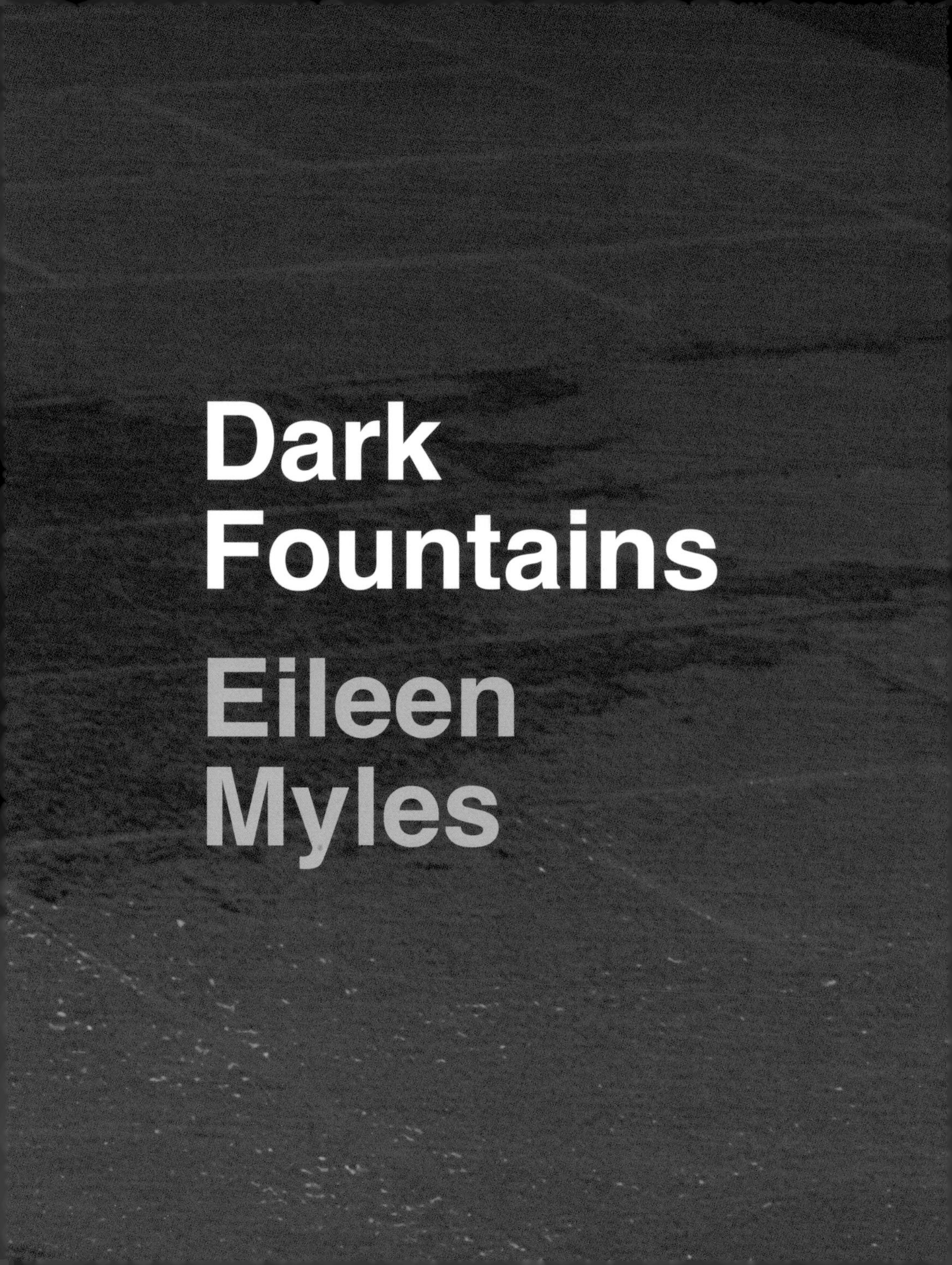
Dark
Fountains
Eileen
Myles

DARK FOUNTAINS

EILEEN MYLES

What's amazing is I start to smell piss. It's more the splotchy dark puddles than the sensational stream of urine that inspires the sensation that I smell piss. One doesn't pee in public without being well aware of the smell. I always piss next to my car at the El Paso airport. There's something about being late for my plane and I really couldn't stop that makes it so pleasurable to drop a big puddle among the cars. But these girls are really impressive in how they've jiggered their cunts for maximum distance performance. It's almost Olympic.

I wonder if they are all the kind of women who go out without panties which I've begun to conclude are most of the women in the world who wear skirts who are quietly sexual or else young. Cause I don't see any panty wringing after these performances. I mean I could say these are exclusively athletic performances of public

VAUXHALL BRIDGE 1995/2013

peeing. I don't know why I've shifted to peeing from pissing. I'll probably shift back in a bit. But the point is that I bet most women squat when they piss between cars etc. There's something both hot and demeaning to see a woman with either her jeans jammed down around her calves and all the pressure on her thigh muscles to hold that squat or else a skirt or a dress yanked up, accordioned around her hips next to a tree or a house or in an alley.

These pissing women (it's back) are all vertical projectile sporting sorts and, for a second, I wanted to suggest that they were trans or that they were surreptitiously using my instrument of choice, a p-style which you jam through the fly of your jeans so that you can swiftly piss – generally alongside your car. It's just so cool to piss anywhere at all in the middle of the day, but these women are night creatures, swift, abundant and proud, well-endowed with great, strong, robust pelvic floor muscles which they can use like this or any way they want. They can leave a dark puddle or they can come. Probably both on any given night. I like them standing with their wide dark production, that three-foot puddle.

I like them accompanied by the cops who may or may not be penalising them for their pissing crime. How often is a man ticketed for urination? I think a cop would be ashamed to do such a thing, unless the man pissing was black and the cop was white and needed to do such a thing. I think it's an attempt to shame. But I see nothing but pride as these women stand by their puddles in the arc of the night, or by the men who are mildly belittled by their failed attempts to make these sculpturally sublime women – these living fountains of urban piss – feel anything but pride . . .

Because there is nothing else and the night is huge, wide, wet and stupendous.

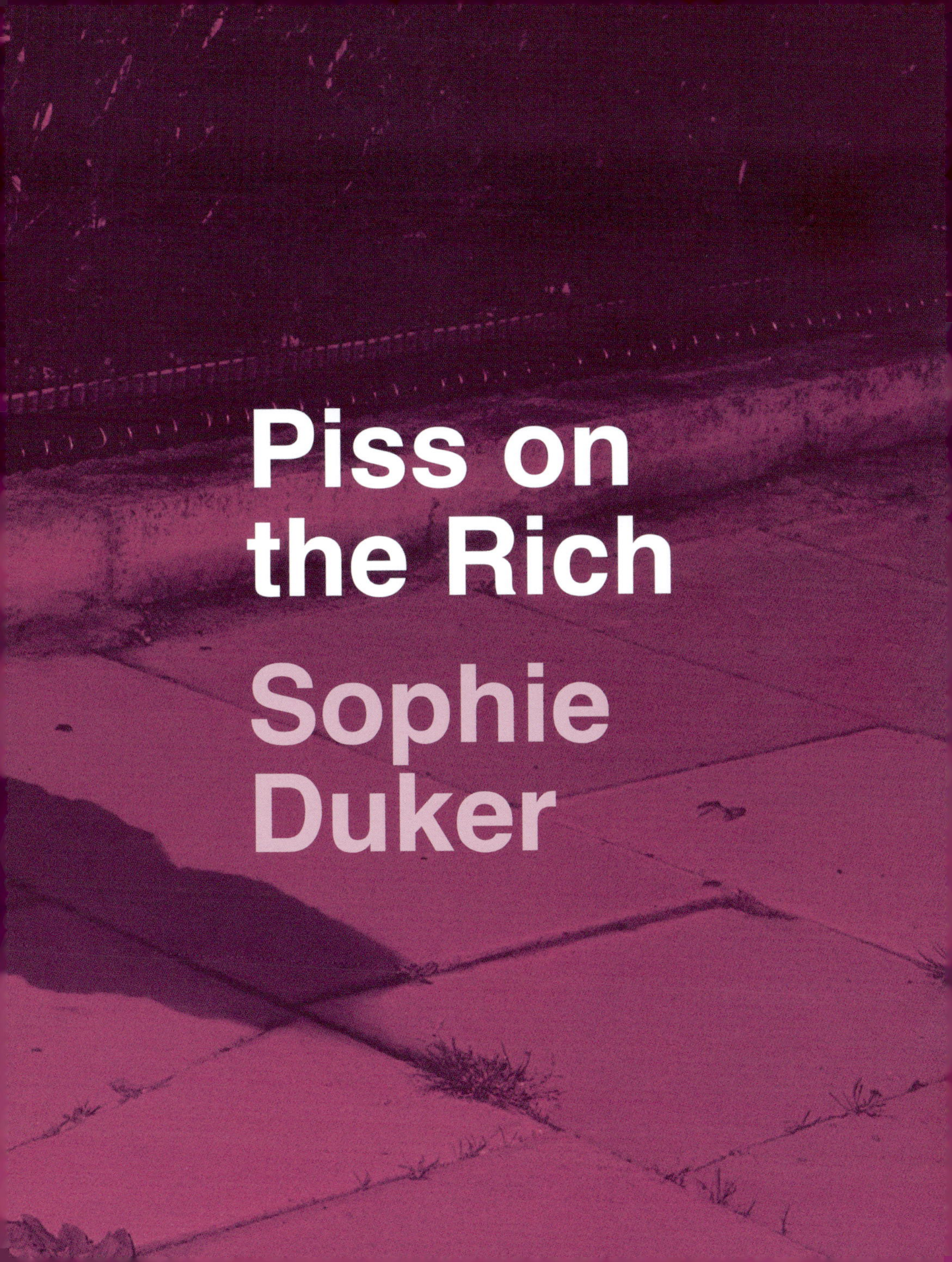

Piss on the Rich

Sophie Duker

PISS ON THE RICH

SOPHIE DUKER

I opened my front door and immediately saw a woman pissing. It was a Sunday morning and I was living in the first of my East London flatshares, four minutes from the Junction, with the 'Roman' shower and 'leaky' ceiling. People used to drop round just cause they were in the area and I loved the romance and spontaneity that came with my address. Rephrase: I loved hosting the afters, and getting long flat loaves of Kurdish bread to line everyone's stomachs at the pre's. I often feel most happy playing host to a never-ending trickle of friends.

But this pissing woman wasn't a friend. I didn't know her. She was about two metres away, squatting with her dress hitched above her hips. I can't remember why I opened the front door, or whether I then walked past to go somewhere or slammed it shut again to give her some privacy.

But I do remember that first split second of inadvertently catching her mid-piss, and that second split second before I reacted of my brain catching up to the oddness of what was happening. She was over 30, black like me, and apparently unbothered to her puss out just metres away from the main road.

Good, I thought, when I saw her.

Keep Dalston weird.

I don't know if admitting this reaction in print reflects positively on me, to be honest. It's tricky to explain exactly why anyone would greet this particular instance of anti-social behaviour with approval. But seeing a stranger wee on my doorstep somehow meant (to me in that moment) that my beloved Dalston might be able to withstand the slow chokehold of gentrification that had already begun, squeezing out the Caribbean hairdressers, the market sellers, the artists. In my eyes, this woman was not a vagrant but a vigilante, at the forefront of the weirdo resistance. My logic: if Dalston still remained a place where women weed in the street in broad daylight, then future gentrifiers might be sufficiently appalled to leave it well alone. I'd be able to live in my dilapidated Hackney palace forever, kept safe from rising rent prices by an admittedly unorthodox moat.

That didn't happen, obviously. One over-full bladder does not a resistance movement make. My rent rose, I moved to a nicer shared house in leafy Stoke Newington, and gritty, piss-soaked Dalston has lost most of its legendary nightspots, while gaining an M&S and a Pret.

While not opposed, I wouldn't say I'm practiced in public urination. It's only ever been an occasional necessity, never a regular feature, and although there certainly will have been moments in my childhood where it happened, my memories of occasional indulging start at university. It was an era littered with house

OUTTAKE FROM VAUXHALL BRIDGE SHOOT

parties, where for a lot of my peers doing lines off the porcelain throne took higher priority than keeping the loo queue moving.

Boys I hung out with used the term 'having a slash' to describe pissing. You can't deny it's a hell of a rebrand, slang that makes even an everyday bodily function sound cool. And maybe appropriately so – like a cold beer on a hot day, a good piss after a long wait is something almost everyone enjoys. Literal release, followed by sweet unburndened relief. If you've ever waited against your will – for the length of a car journey, or the first act of a shit play – you might have let out an orgasm-adjacent sigh when your cheeks finally kissed the toilet seat and you let it all go. Perhaps we should romanticise the act of pissing more, write poetry about it. If blue balls are considered 'a thing' (they aren't) then so should be the blue bladder.

Notting Hill Carnival – a colourful riot of joy, sound, drink and piss. As a black Londoner it's been easy to find a reason to attend most years. At this annual event – which attracts two million revellers across the weekend – businesses bar their doors and Porta-potties are understandably in short supply. Enterprising locals charge £2, £3, sometimes £5 a pop for a piss in their personal lavatories. Another euphemism for pissing is 'spending a penny'. Between whining my waist at various soundsystems, I'd crouch at the edge of the pavement to wazz, smug in the knowledge that I was making a smart financial decision. Who wouldn't rather spend a penny than a fiver?

Being young and skint wasn't the only reason I liked pissing on Notting Hill's cobbles back in the day. I'm from North London and live in East London, so to me, West London was where the poshos lived. As I confessed once on a podcast (because I have no PR training and regularly forget podcasts are listened to by other people eventually) I was very into pissing on rich people's houses. I don't consider myself to be some kind of working-class hero. But I do – for some reason

– feel like peeing in a mews in Ladbroke Grove can be a small, silly act of class defiance. In my first week at my bourgeois collegiate university, a group of friends from my lefty, state-school coded college snuck into the richest right-wing college and pissed in the long grass. As someone who straddles middle-class-ness, marginalisation and a muddle of other unavoidable social and economic identifiers, the easy rebellion of taboo is so seductive.

Piss on the Rich. Drink with the Poor.

I'm into that.

Piss play is a thing. It's not for me, but I imagine some of you might get turned on looking at these photographs. At one London party I attended, the guests were encouraged to try out the consenting human toilet. It didn't arouse me, but I hope it did something for the man whose face I blessed with a golden shower. Maybe my indifference was because the toilet was a cis-man? A gorgeous stripper I met said that they wouldn't mind me pissing on them if we found time later in the night. We never got around to it, but I also wouldn't have minded.

Sophy Rickett's *Pissing Women* is a springboard for the imagination, opening society's eyes to the fact that women are living, breathing, puking, shitting beings. We can be feral and feminine and frightening. We are more than capable of rebelling, whether it's against social norms or complacent spouses. I know that at the time of their first publication, these images were radical – and they remain relevant and arresting today because of the context in which we still live – a world where the bodies of people who experience misogyny are policed and punished for simply doing what bodies do.

Pissing in public, for the artist and her friends, gives them an almost glamorous edge, the dank puddles and fountains incongruous with how effortlessly chic the subjects look. It's another story entirely for the women who piss in public off-camera: the sex worker whose client won't let her use their bathroom, or the person whose medical needs make them incontinent, or the unhoused woman who doesn't give a shit about making a statement and would opt in to plumbing and privacy in a heartbeat.

This joyful revival of *Pissing Women* makes me think – where next? Which lines will be crossed and imaginations expanded when our trans siblings photograph themselves pissing? Will we soon see black, fat, disabled and divergent bodies weeing on white, mainstream gallery walls? I hope so.

To grossly paraphrase Maya Angelou: no one of us can pee till everybody can pee.

But . . .
How ?

Chila Burman in conversation with Darren Biabowe Barnes

BUT . . . HOW?

CHILA BURMAN IN CONVERSATION WITH DARREN BIABOWE BARNES

DBB: What is your immediate response on seeing these images?

CB: The models all look so great. I like her mini skirt, I love that jacket. I like her shoes. How can you even walk in those heels? Christ. I'd break me neck in those. But I like them.

Standing up to piss, though? How is that even possible? They look like they've got willies attached to them, standing up like that.

They're pissing like men, not crouching like women have to do. Was there some . . . device used? It's impossible for girls to wee like that, isn't it?

DBB: That's a sort of biological question. I'm not sure I can really answer . . .

CB: But they're really doing it? Not just acting for the camera?

DBB: Yep, they are actually pissing. In the name of art. It's an artistic statement, isn't it?

CB: But women can't do it standing like that. Unless . . . can they?

DBB: I mean, I have different hardware . . . you may have to ask someone else.

CB: Let's go back to the photos again.

DBB: Good idea.

CB: This one is especially fantastic. The composition of it. I love how her face appears reflected in those tiles. It looks somehow more like a man's face – a reflection of some man's face.

OUTTAKE FROM OLD STREET SHOOT

In fact, if you don't look too closely, she could well be a man in a skirt.

But blimey – how can you actually do that?! I can't get over this.

DBB: It's been argued that these photographs kind of perform the visual language of feminism as it existed back in the 1990s. Do you recognise that in the series at all?

CB: I wouldn't call them feminist statements exactly, because the women in them are pissing like men. It's more like Margaret Thatcher wearing that huge suit to accentuate her shoulders and appear more masculine. To me, it's sort of saying: 'I want to piss like a man'. But why? Why would you want to piss like a man? I've been to the gents millions of times by mistake, millions, and only noticed because it stinks so much.

DBB: Yeah, I hear you.

CB: . . . and they're all leaning backwards in that strange pose? Do men really lean backwards like that when they piss?

DBB: I don't, as far as I've noticed. Though I can't say that it's something I've put a huge amount of thought into.

CB: And this great pool below the model here – has she just weed there?

DBB: She has. That's her wee.

CB: Blimey! How do they get that much out? I don't know how anyone can produce all that piss. I'd like to meet these girls and ask them how they've managed this.

DBB: You'd be surprised how much piss there is on the floors in the gent's toilets. It feels like wading sometimes.

CB: The floor is wet in women's toilets

OUTTAKE FROM SILVERTOWN SHOOT

OUTTAKE FROM SILVERTOWN SHOOT

sometimes, too. The floor is always wet in the loos at McDonald's. I could tell you about all the loos in London, I'm an expert.

DBB: I think that's for the next book, perhaps.

CB: I have a very weak bladder. Which means that, when I go, it's often only a few drops that come out. If you have a weak bladder, that's just the way it is. It's almost like being pregnant. It doesn't take long, though, taking my knickers down and all that. A couple of seconds, probably.

DBB: One of the things I love about this series is how uncannily the models are posed. That's not really what it looks like to take a piss. Certainly not the way I think I do it, or the way the other pissers in the gents look like when they're doing it. That must be a deliberate decision.

CB: This one in Pimlico must have been taken just round the corner from the Tate Britain. Just across the road from the Millbank entrance.

Which reminds me of a good piss story that happened to me.

It was the last night of my installation, *Remembering a Brave New World*, over the Millbank entrance. Must have been February 2021. The piece had been up since November, and was one of the Tate's most popular Winter Commissions. People would trek there during lockdown to see it.

So, I'm there on the last night, and it's bloody freezing. By that time, I knew the security like the back of my hand: they'd always let me pop in to make cups of tea to warm up.

But on this night, the last night, it was a different team staring at me from a window up above. And, although I shouted up that I needed access, they claimed to have been given strict instructions not to let anyone in. I went beserk, going "this is absolutely ridiculous! You've got to let me in!" But no.

And so there I was, freezing cold, bladder full to bursting, standing in front of my own artwork. I had to do something. So, I ran round to the Manton entrance. So fast, in fact, that I tumbled over before I made it.

I couldn't get in there either. None of my shouting or explanations were any good – I had no choice but to take my tiny bladder home in a taxi. Back I went to the Millbank entrance and called one, which ferried me all the way, from west to north London, still desperate.

It was in the cab that I noticed that my hands weren't cold like usual. More than that, there was some horrible pain creeping up my wrist from the fall I'd taken earlier. I knew straightaway that it was serious. All because those jobsworths wouldn't let me piss!

So, I had to call another taxi right as I got home and relieved myself. This time, I was off to the Royal Free for what would turn out to be a fractured wrist. It was put in plaster and everything.

I won't name names but the Tate bigwigs were horrified. They sent me chocolates, and even offered to wash my hair for me – which was a bit odd. I could have kicked up a real fuss.

All for a piss! This would never have happened to a male artist. If they didn't let a male artist in, he would have been able to find a good spot to take a leak. Round by the trees near the Millbank entrance, probably.

So, maybe I've changed my mind, and these photographs are feminist statements after all.

I'll have to practice doing it stood up, though. I really will. Let's have another look.

Yes. I'll have to practice.

Old Street, 1995

Karmic
Twists
Lily Cole

KARMIC TWISTS
LILY COLE

There have long been different rules for men and women, and pissing norms are amongst them. The cultural ambivalence (or outrage) directed at men publicly pissing stands in contrast with the need (and willingness) of women to hide the act.

The image of a man taking a leak in a city is as hard to avoid as advertising. Yet, before seeing the images in *Pissing Women*, how many amongst us have seen a woman publicly piss standing up? Anatomical quandaries may perplex minds at the thought, just as lesbian sex begs straight questions. How would she even do it? The more familiar female pissing image, etched into the collective subconscious of our time, is women lined up in front of the skirted toilet sign.

The invention of the toilet in Western society was arguably one of the stepping stones towards what we today would recognise as 'civilisation', and it is inextricably connected to social class. Indeed, the flushable toilet was invented by the godson of Queen Elizabeth 1. The little cubicle has long been a successful prop in the cultural and psychological denial of our basic biology. To hide the inevitable demands of our urinating, defecating, class-debunking, animal bodies.

Somehow, men largely slip-streamed out of this cultural shaming. Just as the *Free The Nipple* campaign has sought to point out the gender imbalance in society's tolerance for seeing nipples (yes, we have nipples!) *Pissing Women* invites the question: do men have more permission to be animal?

Of course, part of the gender imbalance with pissing is biological. No doubt the penis, with its protruding extension, and swingable nature, makes a much niftier device for pissing publicly than a cavernous vulva with its hidden urethra. You can't so easily direct the urethra with a hand. But as *Pissing Women* clearly demonstrates,

FIRST TEST SHOOT, 1994, LOCATION UNKNOWN

women can – and do – successfully piss standing up. It just requires imagination and a sophisticated hip manoeuvre.

The images in *Pissing Women* were shot in the London city streets: incubator of business, money, work, culture and madness. The photos are taken at night: indicating the clandestine, illicit nature of the act of peeing publicly, whoever you are. Then there are the policemen; reminiscent of the smiling policewoman in Pipilotti Rist's film *Ever Is Over All.* The police are the human faces of what Michel Foucault called 'governmentality': orchestrating, enforcing – and in this case playfully breaking – the rules of this cultural dance. That the police are men, and smiling, brings them in on the joke: allies, even. These photos were taken in 1994, not many years after the Public Order Act made it illegal to urinate in public in the UK.

Finally, let's consider the clothes the *Pissing Women* wear. Fashion has long been a contentious battleground for representations of gender and class. For centuries fashion has been used to display status and gender, and entrench class differences; or conversely to dispel hierarchies, question the status quo, and as a site of feminist struggle. Joan of Arc was burnt at the stake in 1431 for persistently wearing men's clothes. A 1620 pamphlet illustration called 'The Man-Woman' satirized the trend of women to cut their hair short or dress in a masculine style, which both King James I and the clergy were actively trying to discourage. As late as 1919, Puerto Rican labour leader Luisa Capetillo was jailed for wearing trousers.

So, it is notable that the women pissing are wearing office clothes. The fashion of the city workplace: smart, moneyed, and reflecting the (relatively recent) movement of women into work spaces that were marked male territory. These women wear not just any suits, but skirt-suits: skirts that make it all the easier to pee standing up in. What a karmic twist.

The point of *Pissing Women* is of course symbolic. That the photographic series intends to create a mass movement of women pissing in city streets, seems as likely as understanding Rist's *Ever Is Over All* (or Beyonce's homage to it in *Hold Up*) as a clarion call for women to start smashing car windows.

Yet some women enjoy peeing standing. "I used to do it as a child in the garden, and I still do, and I love it," my friend, artist Nat Sly, tells me. "In the land in the summer, it's my favourite thing in the world just to open my legs and pee standing up."

Perhaps part of the enduring cult resonance of *Pissing Women* three decades on comes from it speaking to some nascent, anarchic desire in men and women alike to feel the primal liberation of pissing as our ancestors might have. Like the experience of goosebumps, freely pissing offers an embodied reminder that underneath the civilising veneers of suits, skirts, city streets, police uniforms and all the other paraphernalia of governmentality, and beyond different gendered rules for culturally acceptable behaviour, we are all fundamentally, and equally, animal.

OUTTAKE FROM SILVERTOWN SHOOT

Revisiting What It Means to Be a Girl

Annie Clark aka St. Vincent in conversation with Sophy Rickett

REVISITING WHAT IT MEANS TO BE A GIRL ANNIE CLARK AKA ST. VINCENT IN CONVERSATION WITH SOPHY RICKETT

ANNIE CLARK (AC) Is it okay if I start by geeking out on *Pissing Women*!? We paid homage to the series on the gatefold of my last record, *All Born Screaming*, I love it so much.

The set for our version uses a street corner – a liminal kind of space. I developed the concept with my friend and collaborator, the artist Alex Da Corte. Elementally, we chose fire for the front cover. And, because it's always good to have balance we felt that there needed to be a water element on the inside.

SOPHY RICKETT (SR) Where did you first encounter the series?

AC: When we were thinking about the campaign for the album, Alex and I went through this process of visiting galleries, watching films, and searching for that something which called out to us and the themes of the record. I fell in love with so many things he showed me – the whole process in fact felt sort of supernatural. Emotional.

I think I saw *Pissing Women* for the very first time then, in one of the many books Alex keeps in his studio in Philadelphia.

SR: I love the set, the street scene. There is something Edward Hopper about it.

And you've nailed the gesture perfectly! Arched back, leaning slightly away. It's such a distinctive gesture; conveys a real attitude. You have appropriated it beautifully.

AC: I looked at the camera though, which I'm not sure you did in the original set of photographs.

SR: You're right. It was important to me that our expressions were completely deadpan, like we were doing something totally normal, simply a part of the everyday urban experience – which it is for a lot of men, at least it was at the time.

AC: Perfectly as it should be . . . !

How did the series come about? It wasn't long after you left art college, right?

SR: The idea first arrived in the summer, 1994.

I was at Glastonbury, which felt a world away from my day job as a temp for the *Financial Times,* which consisted almost entirely of photocopying, faxing documents, and posting out CD-Roms.

My friend and fellow artist Rut Blees Luxembourg had a similar job nearby. We'd meet after office hours and wonder how, having just finished at art school, we'd wound up in the strange and alien corporate world.

FROM THE SERIES *CHANCE ENCOUNTERS* (1995) BY RUT BLEES LUXEMBURG.

We wanted to put to test a theory we'd been introduced to during our studies: namely, the idea that gestures of dissent are more powerful when they come from *within* an institution, rather than from the outside.

Rut was studying for her MA and developing

FROM THE SERIES *CHANCE ENCOUNTERS* (1995) BY RUT BLEES LUXEMBURG.

a new project titled *Chance Encounters*. This involved us photographing each other initiating encounters with city workers, taking an exaggeratedly dominant role as women.

I, meanwhile, was in the early stages of the series of photographs that would eventually become

Pissing Women. At the end of the working day, Rut and I would meet with our cameras and explore the City of London – and the hypermasculine areas around Aldgate, Liverpool Street, and Bishopsgate in particular.

At the start, we tried to select locations to shoot that were discrete and less likely to attract the attention of passersby to begin with but, as our confidence grew, we came to realise that our performances needed to be out in the open, visible to the public.

The documentary-style staging was a part of that – the sense of the photographs capturing something real, or at least viable.

AC: And what about the outfits? You talked about observing these men from the financial district – these people who basically run the UK economy – not just pissing, but pissing with an attitude of '*I'm in an expensively tailored suit and I'm peeing on the pavement.*'

SR: Exactly! Just like it was with the locations, our outfits are a combination of staging and circumstance. We spent most of our money back then on two things: photography and rent. My friend Becky Earley (now a Textile Designer at University Arts London) had recently graduated from Central Saint Martins and if I needed something other than my usual look of charity shop suits and trainers, she'd happily let me borrow something from her.

The shoes we're wearing in the series were samples, lent by Nicky Lawler. At the time, we imagined that the suit I'm wearing on Vauxhall Bridge looked like Vivienne Westwood, but it resolutely was not. More like £2 from a charity shop, and full of moth holes – a 25-year old's understanding of corporate attire, basically. A little bit off.

AC: Perfectly so. If your appearance was too coiffed, it would look more like an *Italian Vogue* shoot or something. It wouldn't have landed.

SR: After the photographs were first exhibited in 1995, I received offers to shoot the series 'properly'; to make a book of them and work with a stylist, professional hair and makeup, studio lighting.

But the series reflects such a specific time, before digital retouching became mainstream. It wouldn't work in the same way now. Digital manipulation smooths everything out. It's reductive, too perfect.

I think that if *Pissing Women* was released today, people would assume they were AI-generated, or Photoshopped. The reality was that we were a group of friends hanging out, making art. It was OK for things to be a bit rough around the edges.

AC: I think that is the best ethos when making art with your friends.

SR: I've always been drawn to working collaboratively. I love the shared dialogue. Any situation can be productive when approached with the right person.

The photographic work we made during those years was fundamentally enabled by the routine of our day jobs, and the discussions we'd have about them when we met for lunch in the office canteen. Instead of pushing that reality away, we posed as corporate insiders, embracing the environment as an influence. A pair of outwardly obedient secretaries on a mission to disrupt!

AC: *Pissing Women* is incredibly — what's the word I'm looking for? — *transgressive*. Not in a showy or contrived way. But in the way the clothes, the locations, the postures are all carefully considered.

SR: Ever since their first publication, the series had only ever consisted of three photographs – the MI6 building seen from Vauxhall Bridge representing the culture of security and surveillance; the British Telecom satellite dishes in Silvertown representing flow of information and global communication; the marble cladding in Old Street representative of the corporate environment.

In 2023, I was approached by Isabella Burley with the idea of publishing the series in its entirety, outtakes and all. I was concerned initially that seeing the series in its entirety might reduce the impact of the original three images but actually found that so much more is revealed than I'd anticipated.

AC: Can you give an example?

SR: Well, to start with: that puddle! It seems so much more transgressive without the presence of the female subject than it ever had before – seeing the puddle in isolation bought it more squarely into the frame.

AC: Is more transgressive than the act itself...? You seem to be saying: *'Hey — fucking walk through it. Deal with it!'*

OUTTAKE FROM SILVERTOWN SHOOT

After the series was first released, were there a lot of eyes on you? Did you feel any pressure to come out with something equally subversive? Were you thinking where to go from there?

SR: The photographs were exhibited for the first time in Plummet Gallery, a small artist-run space in London set up by Billy Shoebridge. The show was called *Stream*, and was organised by the three exhibiting artists – Rut, our mutual friend Carey Young, and me.

It was the first time I'd exhibited my work outside college, and the reaction was amazing. There were reviews in *Time Out*, *Creative Camera* and the newly-inaugurated *Mute Magazine*. As exciting as it was, looking back, I'm not sure I was ready. It was a bit too much.

The internet was in its early days during 1995. Email and file-sharing were just beginning to infiltrate mainstream culture, and soon after that first exhibition my photographs started springing up in unexpected places: 'golden shower' fetish websites and blogs; the Swedish daily newspaper *Aftonbladet*; on a sticker stuck to a lamppost in Soho advertising a club night.

I tried to ignore the pressure about what was next and carried on in a similar vein for a few years, before enrolling onto a postgraduate degree at the Royal College of Art in 1997.

Most of my work from that time was inspired by the city environment. My 24-hour staff security pass to the *Financial Times* offices offered me a rare level of access, which in turn enabled me to produce several series of photographs, as well as a short video work where an impromptu performance was filmed using the FT's network of nighttime security cameras.

In the photography series *Office Interiors*, I took some friends into the building in the middle of the night and staged a series of tableau style portraits in the open plan offices. The fluorescent ceiling lights would be left on all night, so after dark the windows — which during the day framed sweeping views of the Thames and St Pauls Cathedral — became mirrors, and as a worker there myself, I felt implicated. I felt part of the corporate condition.

AC: Do you have a hard time looking back on certain pieces, ones you made a long time ago? Do they still resonate? It might have done at the time, but differently?

Put differently, do you ever have trouble making peace with earlier iterations of yourself?

SR: Once a piece of work is released into the world, it can be difficult for the artist to retrieve its meaning or to re-define it. This feels even more true in the age of the internet, and our culture of cut-and-paste . . . creative work is never made in a silo.

When the context around something changes,

the sense of it does as well.

AC: Yes, absolutely. This many records in and also being a new mother has given me a new lens to view my experience and has inspired more compassion in me for my younger self and the things I was trying to do. Far more than I had at the time.

I found it hard to have compassion for my younger self in any kind of way until I was able to externalise the condition of being a young person or girl. I have endless compassion for my daughter: why not for an earlier iteration of myself?

You must be used to doing interviews about your work, for publications or on camera, or being asked to explain things in writing.

Do you feel compelled to make your work make sense to new audiences? To account for a sense of progression? How different is the work you make now to the work you made back then?

TEST SHOOT AT BROADGATE CIRCLE

SR: In the past, I've felt the need to account for certain shifts in my work, though I experience that less now. I recognise the continuity running through what I do and have done in a more nuanced way.

Looking back, although I didn't have the language for it at the time, I can see in my early work an interest in how our environments shape and condition us, and a desire to propose alternative modes of behaviour, or models of resistance. That concern is ongoing, though my practice has evolved both in relation to the visual form it takes, and my methodological approach.

Writing has become more central, and now most of my projects involve sustained research into specific cultural sites to explore the relationship between landscape, photography, heritage, and place.

But the echoes of *Pissing Women* remain. I am still very much interested in the condition and representation of the 'feminine', and in exploring how identities are formed, restrained, contorted and supported, though perhaps employing more subtle visual strategies than I did when I was 25.

AC: And anyway . . . if the work is good enough, no story is required outside of it. In certain situations, it might need to be packaged up, or bullet pointed. But the hope is always that the work doesn't need to explain itself. That it doesn't require a placard to be weird or confrontational and *Pissing Women* is both of those things – it has an intensity and a level of violence, while also being deeply funny.

OUTTAKE FROM VAUXHALL BRIDGE SHOOT

Contributors

HETTIE JUDAH
CRITIC

Hettie Judah is an art critic and curator. Her writing is regularly featured in *The Guardian*, the *Times Literary Supplement* and *Frieze*, and she can be heard on BBC 4's Front Row. *Acts of Creation: On Art and Motherhood*, a Hayward Gallery Touring exhibition curated by Judah, was launched alongside her book of the same name at the Arnolfini, Bristol, in 2024.

PATRICIA NILSSON
JOURNALIST

Patricia Nilsson is a *Financial Times* journalist and podcaster. Her work has seen her cover a broad range of industries, from tobacco and cannabis to pornography. The host of the *Financial Times*' hugely successful first narrative podcast series, *Hot Money*, Nilsson is currently working on her debut book-length investigation, which will be published by Allen Lane.

JUNO CALYPSO
PHOTOGRAPHER

Juno Calypso is an artist and photographer whose work has been exhibited and enjoyed critical acclaim globally. One of the most recognisable living fine art photographers, Calypso's self-portraits are held in esteemed public collections like the Wellcome Collection and the Manchester Art Gallery.

HOLLY BLAKEY
CHOREOGRAPHER

Holly Blakey is a choreographer and dancer whose work straddles live performance and film. Blakey's work as both a director and choreographer has seen her collaborate with artists such as Rosalia, Harry Styles and Florence and the Machine (for which she was awarded an MVA for 'Best Choreography in a Video'), as well as fashion houses such as Burberry, Dior, and Gucci. Her collaborations with Mica Levi, the London Contemporary Orchestra and Vivienne Westwood, *Cowpuncher My Ass*, ran for five years, closing at a sold-out Royal Festival Hall in 2020.

SOPHIE FIENNES
DIRECTOR

Sophie Fiennes is a director whose innovative non-fiction films have been broadcast and screened globally. With work spanning installation art (*current/SEE*, Tate) to collaborations with the philosopher Slavoj Zizek (*The Pervert's Guide to Cinema* and *The Pervert's Guide to Ideology*), Fiennes' singular and ground-breaking approach to cinema has stunned audiences at Sundance, Rotterdam, Cannes and more.

EILEEN MYLES
POET

Eileen Myles is a New York-based poet and novelist. Widely regarded as one of the most recognised and forward-thinking writers of their generation, Myles is the recipient of a number of prestigious awards, including the Guggenheim, and was inducted into the American Academy of Arts & Letters in 2022.

SOPHIE DUKER
COMEDIAN

Sophie Duker is a comedian and writer. Now a regular on nationally broadcast panel shows, including Frankie Boyle's *New World Order*, Duker's Edinburgh Fringe Show, Venus, saw her nominated for the Best Newcomer Award and led to a sold-out run at the Soho Theatre, London.

CHILA BURMAN
ARTIST

Chila Burman MBE is an internationally exhibited artist and printmaker. Her work has been shown in notable public institutions such as the British Council, the V&A Museum, the BFI and Tate Britain, Tate Modern and Tate Liverpool. She was awarded an MBE in the Queen's Birthday Honours in 2022 for services to visual art.

LILY COLE
ACTOR

Lily Cole is an actor, director, model and activist. The recipient of an honorary doctorate from the University of Glasgow, Cole is additionally an advisor to the United Nations ECE's Sustainability Pledge.

ST. VINCENT
MUSICIAN

Anne Erin Clark, known professionally as St. Vincent, is an American musician, singer and songwriter. Her guitar playing has been praised for its melodic style and use of distortion, and she has been listed among the best guitarists of the 21st century by multiple publications. *Rolling Stone* named Clark the 26th-greatest guitarist of all time in 2023.

SOPHY RICKETT
PHOTOGRAPHER

Sophy Rickett is an award-winning artist and writer whose work has been exhibited internationally, including at the Victoria and Albert Museum, London, and the Centre Pompidou, Paris. Her work is held in major public and private collections such as the UK Government Art Collection and the Federal Reserve, Washington D.C. It has also been featured in mainstream media outlets including *The Observer* and *Libération*. Her ground-breaking series *Pissing Women* (1995) was first published in a limited-edition monograph by Climax Books (2023). In addition to her artistic practice, she is a Reader at the University of the Arts London.

ACKNOWLEDGEMENTS FROM THE ARTIST

I would like to thank everyone who has supported this project over the years including . . . Becky Earley, Nicky Lawler, Lena Corner and Sasha Portis.

Many thanks to Isabella Burley for coming up with the idea of bringing the images together for the Climax Books edition, 2023.

It has been a joy working with the team at CHEERIO Publishing – Darren, Labeja, Clare, Tiana, Elizabeth and Harriet – and I couldn't be more grateful that such an incredibly diverse array of talented women have shared their responses to the work.

Deepest gratitude as ever to Rut Blees Luxemburg and Carey Young for your friendship and support.

Sophy Rickett, 2025